What are Monk's Cloth Afghans?

These afghans are created by running a needle and yarn along the surface of a material called monk's cloth. This fabric has a distinct weave of four vertical and four horizontal threads per block (**Fig 1**). The yarn is slipped behind the blocks of vertical threads to create a design according to the pattern followed. All of the "stitching" appears on the top of the fabric and rarely shows through to the back.

Fig 1

Here's What You'll Need

The Yarn
The yarn used to make a monk's cloth afghan is traditional 4-ply worsted weight acrylic yarn.

The Needle
Use a #13 metal yarn needle for stitching monk's cloth afghans. You will also need a measuring tape, a pair of scissors, and some safety pins.

Monk's Cloth
Monk's cloth is available in white, natural, black, and a variety of other colors. It is 59" to 60" wide. This cloth has an interesting texture due to its distinctive weave: four vertical and four horizontal threads that create blocks. By slipping yarn behind the blocks of vertical threads at prescribed intervals (see Photo A below), a design can be created.

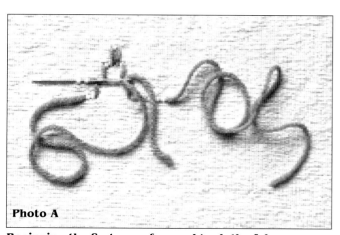

Photo A

Beginning the first row of a monk's cloth afghan.

The Stitches

When stitching, the blocks of vertical th stitch with a detaile or left to right if you are left-handed. The needle does not go through to the back side of the cloth. Simply slip the needle under the vertical blocks of threads.

Straight Stitch
This is the basic stitch; all the others are variations.

Stitch **under** a block of vertical threads and **over** the horizontal threads to form a straight stitch (**Fig 2**).

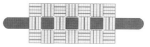

Fig 2

Slant Stitch Up
Bring the yarn out of the last block of vertical threads shown in the pattern, then go up to the row indicated and under the first vertical block to continue the pattern (**Fig 3**).

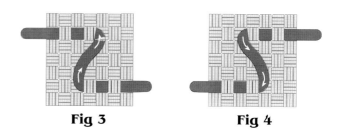

Fig 3   **Fig 4**

Slant Stitch Down
This stitch is the same as the Slant Stitch Up but worked in the opposite direction (**Fig 4**). Bring the yarn out of the last block of vertical threads shown in the pattern, then go down to the row indicated and under the first vertical block to continue pattern.

Short Slant Stitch
This is worked in the same manner as the more traditional Slant Stitches above, but the length of each stitch is shorter (**Fig 5**). This stitch is used for the diamond pattern described on pages 6 and 7.

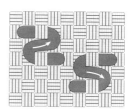

Fig 5

1

V Stitch

To begin stitch, go under only two vertical threads on the right half of the bottom block. Bring yarn up to the block indicated in the pattern and go under all four threads, bring yarn back down and under the remaining two threads of the bottom block (**Fig 6**).

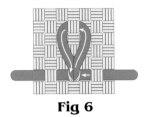

Fig 6

X Stitch

Bring yarn under the vertical block at center of stitch, then up over rows indicated on chart and under three vertical blocks at top of stitch (**Fig 7**). Bring yarn back under center vertical block but over the top of previous yarn. Go down rows indicated on chart and under three vertical blocks at bottom of stitch. Bring yarn back under center vertical block but over the previous yarn to complete stitch.

Fig 7

The Charts

The stitches are worked in continuous rows on the afghan. Each row is always worked in the same color; there will not be a "stop and start" in the middle of a row to switch to a new color.

Each design is charted, with lines indicating the colors and stitches to be worked. In the charts, the yarn colors are represented by black lines of various thicknesses.

Each chart shows only the vertical blocks. The lines on the chart represent the visible yarn. Below are examples of the different stitches and how they appear on our charts.

Straight Stitch

Slant Stitch Up

Slant Stitch Down

Short Slant Stitch

V Stitch

X Stitch

Cloth Amount and Preparation

A lap throw or baby afghan will require one yard of monk's cloth. The **height** of the finished project will run from selvage to selvage and measure about 30" wide by 50" high. A larger sofa throw or bed afghan will require two yards of monk's cloth. The **width** of the finished project will run from selvage to selvage and will measure about 50" wide by 65" high.

Monk's cloth does require a certain amount of preparation before beginning to stitch. It ravels quite easily and shrinks when washed, as it is 100% cotton.

To prepare monk's cloth for stitching:

1. Remove enough threads from the cut edges of the fabric until there is a continuous thread all the way across. Trim off excess threads but **do not** cut to desired finished size at this time.
2. Machine stitch (zigzag is preferable) two rows of stitches, or hand baste a hem to prevent the cut ends from raveling.
3. Machine wash and rinse in cold water and use fabric softener if desired. Dry flat or in a dryer at medium or low heat. There will be shrinkage; this is desirable because the yarn will fit the fabric weave better and the fabric becomes softer.
4. Now hem the side edges. For a lap throw or baby afghan, turn under three, then five rows of the cut edges (**Fig 8**). Pin in place and baste by hand, keeping your stitches fairly loose and spacing them two or three blocks apart. If you are making a sofa throw or bed afghan, fold the selvages over the width of five or six rows and baste by hand.

Hem side edges.

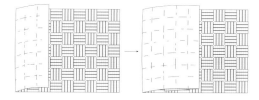

Fig 8

5. Leave the top and bottom edges of the afghan unhemmed at this time. This will allow for any size adjustment that might be needed after stitching.

Yarn

Traditional 4-ply worsted weight acrylic yarn was used to make these afghans. Choose your favorite colors to coordinate with a room's decor or use the colors shown in our patterns.

These designs can be stitched more quickly than other monk's cloth afghans and less yarn is needed due to the open diamond pattern. No more than one 3-ounce skein of each color is needed, even for the larger size.

Start in the Middle

It is very important to always stitch from the center of the afghan out to its sides in order to keep the fabric from becoming distorted or off grain. After preparing the cloth as described on page 3, find the center of the afghan. To determine the center, fold the afghan into quarters, carefully matching the corners and sides. Mark the center using a safety pin.

You may want to double check the center location by laying out the cloth flat and measuring. The design pattern will indicate if the center knot needs to be tied over a block of horizontal or vertical threads. In the same block as your safety pin, tie a loose yarn knot using one or two strands of a contrasting color from your stitching colors (**Fig 9**), then remove the pin. The pin can snag your yarn or cloth, and you will be frequently using the center knot as a reference point.

Fig 9

Remember! To keep your afghan from becoming distorted, always start in the center of the fabric to stitch one half of the row, then stitch the other half. Never start at one side and stitch all the way across to the other side.

Beginning to Stitch

The length of yarn required is given for each row in a pattern and is measured by using the width of the afghan. For example, 2W means to use a piece of yarn twice the width of the fabric. 2½W means a piece of yarn two and one half times the width of the fabric. Lay the yarn on top of the fabric and straighten it to measure, but do not stretch the yarn.

While stitching, it is important to keep the tension on the yarn even. Pulling too tight will pucker the fabric, and too loose will make the work look sloppy. Make the first few stitch(es) as directed in the individual pattern instructions (see Photo B below). Place the two ends of the yarn together and gently pull the yarn through the fabric until you have divided its length in half. Leave the right half off to the side. If you are left-handed work the opposite way.

Photo B

Following the pattern, stitch with the left half of the yarn from the middle of the afghan toward the left, repeating the pattern until reaching the fourth or fifth block from the edge. Slide the needle down through the fabric and hide the yarn inside the hem bringing it out of the fold at the afghan edge (see Photo C below).

Photo C

Turn the afghan around (top to bottom). Pick up the remaining half of the yarn and stitch the other half of the row (see Photo D below).

Photo D

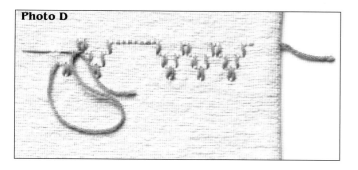

Continue stitching each row in its entirety, always starting in the center.

Tips and Hints

When stitching your afghan, support your cloth on a table or over a firm pillow on your lap. This will help control the tension and make placing your stitches easier.

If a stitch is pulled too tightly, looks too short, or buries itself in the fabric, slip the tip of your needle under the stitch from above and lift the yarn to adjust it.

Check your progress often to be sure you are stitching the pattern correctly, especially when there is a change in the pattern shape.

If a mistake is found, remove the needle from the yarn and use the tip of the needle to draw up a small loop until you can grasp it. Gently pull the yarn back out of the fabric and remove small sections at a time so you don't distort the fabric. Be sure you have the needle under all strands of the yarn before lifting it up.

Diamond Afghan Planning

Each design consists of three parts: a center motif, a diamond section, and an end motif (**Fig 10**). The center and end motifs are charted on the individual project pages, but the pattern chart for the diamond section is shown on the opposite page because it is the same for all eight afghans.

Fig 10

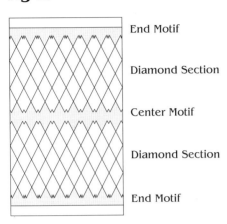

End Motif

Diamond Section

Center Motif

Diamond Section

End Motif

Each project provides instruction for a small throw or a large afghan. To make a size different than the one specified, a little planning is necessary before stitching to know how many diamond rows are needed.

Follow these steps:

Step 1: Prepare the monk's cloth as described on page 3.

Step 2: Select a pattern and tie the center knot on a vertical or horizontal block (depending on the pattern), following the instructions on page 4.

Step 3: Count the number of fabric rows from the center knot to the bottom of the afghan. Place a safety pin every 25 rows to help keep your place. Stop counting 3" from bottom edge for hemmed, blanket stitched, or crocheted finish. Stop 4" from bottom edge for fringed finish.

Step 4: The project instructions include the number of fabric rows needed for the end motif and half the center motif. Subtract these two figures from the total rows counted in Step 3.

Step 5: Now determine how many sets of diamond rows are needed to fill the area between the center and end motifs. Each diamond row (A and B) is 31 fabric rows high. However, it is

important to realize that the V Stitch in the valley of Row A goes through the same block of threads in the V Stitch at the peak of Row B (see chart on opposite page). This means that Row A and Row B share one block of threads. This is also true of the V Stitches in the center and end motifs that meet the V Stitches in the diamond rows. In each project pattern, the connecting V Stitches of the diamond rows are charted and labeled to help you keep your place while stitching. **Fig 11** illustrates a typical motif and diamond row placement.

Fig 11

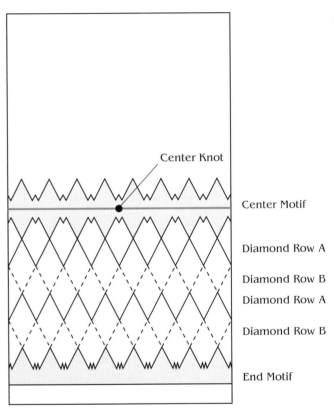

Center Knot

Center Motif

Diamond Row A

Diamond Row B

Diamond Row A

Diamond Row B

End Motif

Step 6: In order for the motifs to meet properly with the diamond rows, the two diamond rows must be stitched as a set. In other words, if two Row A are stitched, you must also stitch two Row B. Determine how many sets of diamond rows you can fit between the center and end motifs.

Step 7: Begin stitching half the center motif from the center knot. Stitch the number of diamond rows needed, then stitch the end motif. Turn cloth top to bottom. Stitch the remaining half of the center motif, the same number of diamond rows, and the end motif. Finish sides and ends as desired; there are several options on page 8.

Diamond Rows

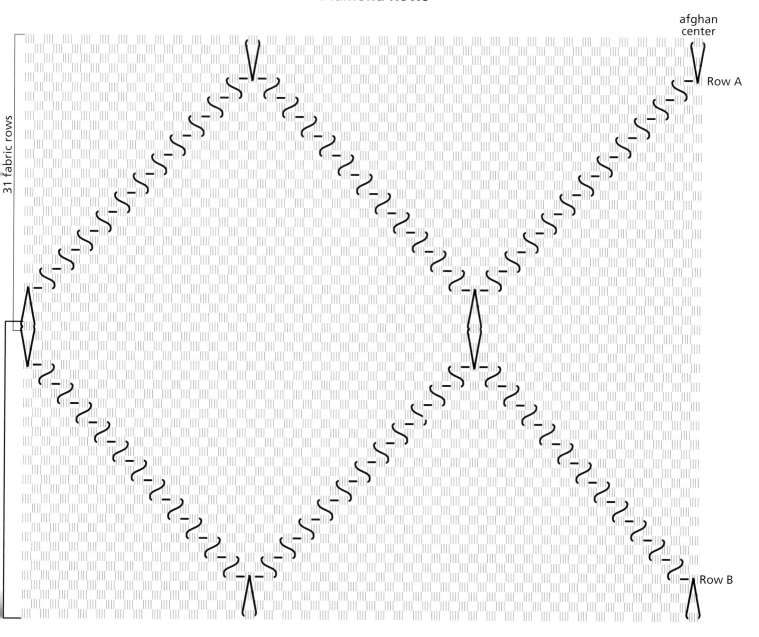

Use yarn color
specified in individual
project instructions.

7

Finishing

When the stitching is complete, here are four options for finishing your afghan.

Hemmed Edges

Using an iron, press the hems for the top and bottom edges the same as the sides. With a sewing machine, stitch around all four hand-basted sides of the afghan.

Holding each individual strand of yarn that extends from the outer edge of the side hems, depress the outer edge slightly and carefully cut off the excess yarn. The cut end of the yarn will be hidden within the hem.

Self Fringe

Machine stitch the two sides and remove the excess ends of yarn as described above.

On the top and bottom of the afghan, machine sew with a zigzag stitch just above the length of fringe desired. Unravel the fabric up to the stitching (**Fig 12**). To straighten the kinked fringe, mist it with water and gently comb with a large toothed comb. Let dry flat or hang.

Fig 12

Blanket Stitch Edging

Machine stitch the two side hems, fold and stitch the hems for the two remaining sides, and remove the excess ends of yarn as described above in Hemmed Edges.

Choose a color of yarn to coordinate with your design. With the same yarn needle used for stitching, make a blanket stitch around the outer edges, spacing the stitches two rows in and two blocks apart (**Fig 13**).

Fig 13

Single Crochet Edging

Machine stitch the two side hems, fold and stitch the hems for the top and bottom, and remove the excess ends of yarn as described at left in Hemmed Edges.

Use a crochet hook, size steel 2 or aluminum B. Insert hook into an intersection, two rows from the hemmed edge. Draw a yarn loop through the fabric, then hook the yarn and draw through the loop (**Fig 14**).

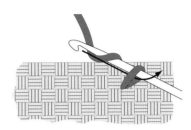

Fig 14

Insert the hook into the fabric two blocks to the left, hook the yarn, and draw through the fabric. Hook the yarn and draw through both loops on the hook to make the first crochet stitch (**Fig 15**).

Fig 15

Insert the hook into the fabric two more blocks to the left, hook the yarn, and draw through both loops again for the second stitch (**Fig 16**). Continue in this manner around the afghan edges. Hide ends inside hem.

Fig 16

Jewel

MATERIALS FOR A LARGE AFGHAN
two yards monk's cloth
tan, gold, and rose worsted weight yarn
      (one 3 ounce skein of each color)
#13 metal yarn needle
measuring tape
safety pin
scissors

INSTRUCTIONS
Prepare monk's cloth as described on page 3. For a smaller afghan, refer to page 6 to plan the number of diamond rows needed. From the center knot, half of the center motif uses 15 fabric rows and the end motifs each use 124 fabric rows.

Place center knot over a block of horizontal threads; see page 4. Start with tan yarn and stitch Row 1 of center motif. Stop stitching at the side a few rows from the hem and hide yarn end as described on page 4 (see Photo C). Stop in same place in the pattern on the opposite side.

After stitching Rows 1—3 of the center motif, stitch the diamond rows using gold and following chart on page 7. Stitch two diamond Row A and two diamond Row B.

Work the end motif, Rows 1—34 as charted on pages 10 and 11. Note that the chart for the end motif is turned sideways and cut in half. The last two rows of cloth at the bottom of the first portion are shaded gray at the top of the second portion. Be sure Rows 21 and 22 fit up into the spaces on first portion.

Turn cloth top to bottom. Stitch the remaining half of the center motif, the same number of diamond rows, and the end motif.

If necessary, trim ends of cloth so the same number of rows border the end motifs at the top and bottom. Finish edges as desired; several methods are described on page 8.

Row	Length	Color
Center Motif		
1	2W	tan
2	3W	gold
3	3¼W	rose
Diamond Section (see page 7)		
A	3W	gold
B	3W	gold

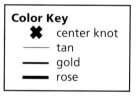

Color Key
✖ center knot
—— tan
—— gold
—— rose

Center Motif (one half)

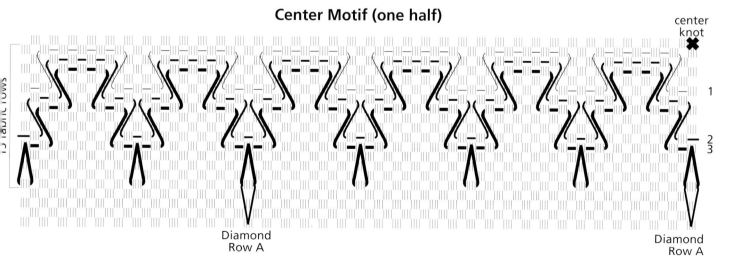

center knot

Diamond Row A

Diamond Row A

continued

End Motif

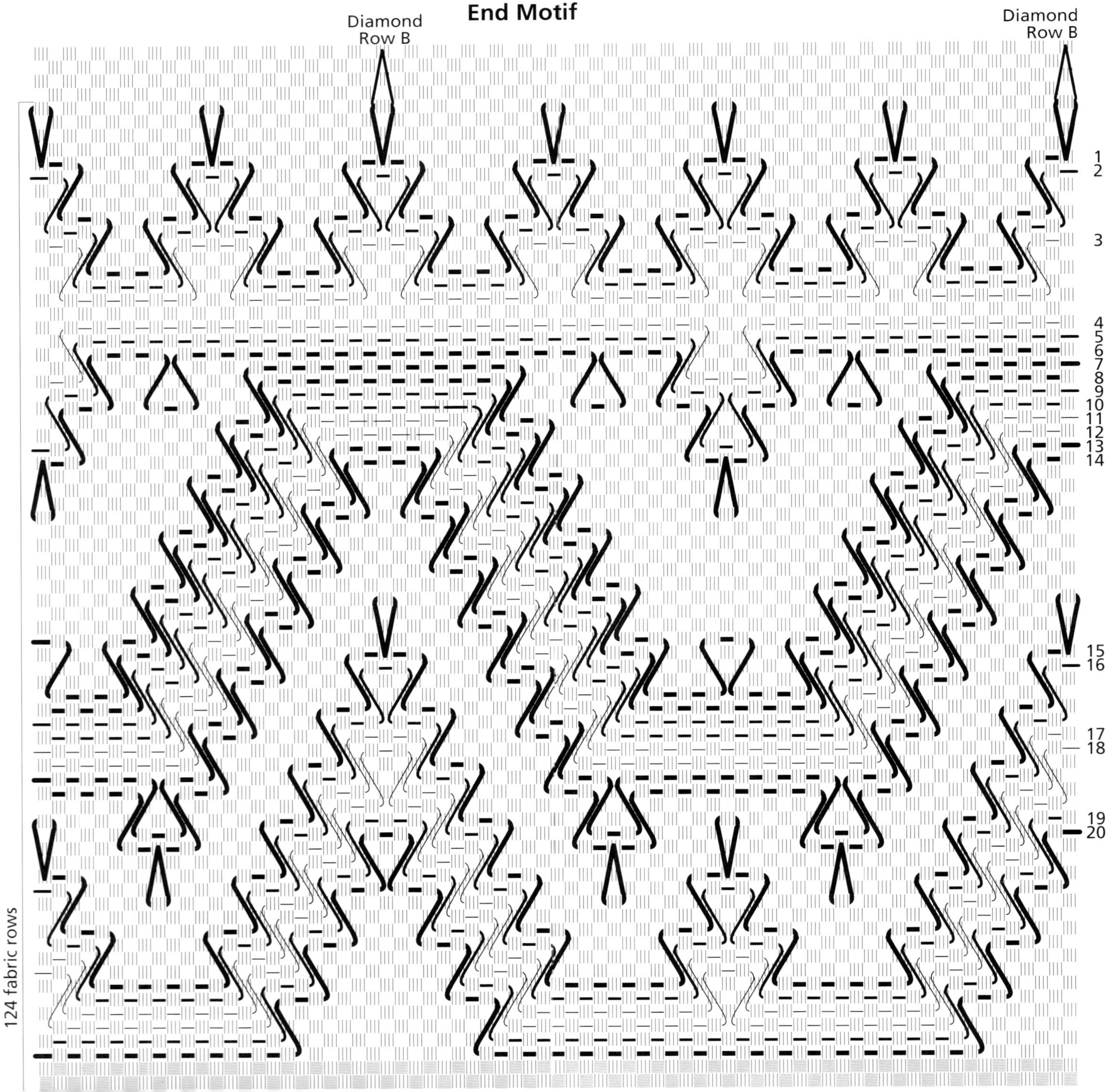
Diamond Row B
Diamond Row B
1
2
3
4
5
6
7
8
9
10
11
12
13
14
15
16
17
18
19
20
124 fabric rows

Color Key

- ✖ center knot
- tan
- gold
- rose

Row	Length	Color
End Motif		
1	3¼W	rose
2	3W	gold
3	2W	tan
4	1½W	tan
5	2W	gold
6	2¼W	rose
7	2½W	rose
8	2½W	rose
9	2½W	gold
10	2½W	gold
11	2¼W	tan
12	2¼W	tan
13	2½W	rose
14	3W	rose
15	3W	rose
16	2½W	gold
17	2½W	tan
18	2¼W	tan
19	2W	gold
20	2W	rose
21	1½W	rose
22	1½W	gold
23	1½W	rose
24	3¼W	rose
25	3W	gold
26	2W	tan
27	2W	tan
28	3W	gold
29	3¼W	rose
30	1½W	rose
31	2¼W	gold
32	2½W	rose
33	2½W	rose
34	2¼W	gold

shaded rows are last two shaded rows on previous page

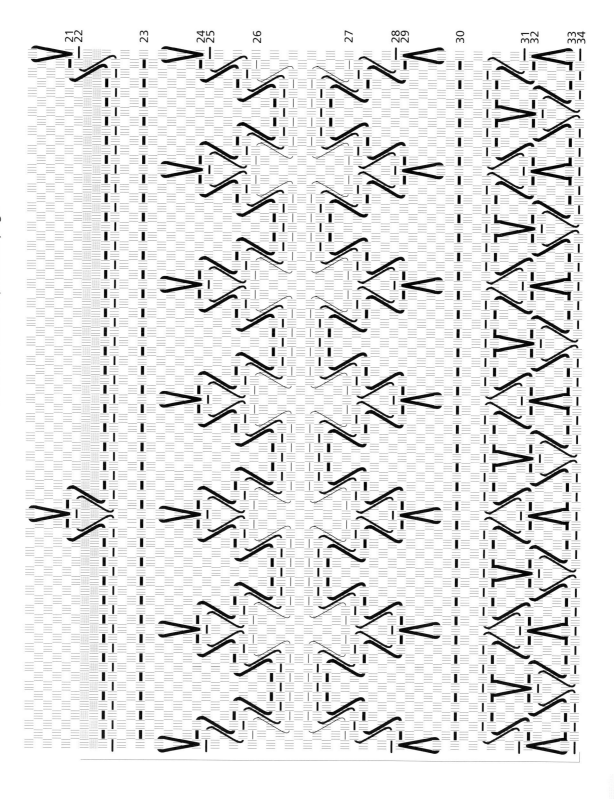

Marquise

MATERIALS FOR A LARGE AFGHAN
two yards monk's cloth
lt pink, med pink, and dk pink worsted weight yarn
      (one 3 ounce skein of each color)
#13 metal yarn needle
measuring tape
safety pin
scissors

INSTRUCTIONS
Prepare monk's cloth as described on page 3. For a smaller afghan, refer to page 6 to plan the number of diamond rows needed. From the center knot, half the center motif uses 21 fabric rows and the end motifs each use 106 fabric rows.

Place center knot over a block of horizontal threads; see page 4. Start with dk pink yarn and stitch Row 1 of center motif. Stop stitching at the side a few rows from the hem and hide yarn end as described on page 4 (see Photo C). Stop in same place in the pattern on the opposite side.

After stitching Rows 1—5 of the center motif, stitch the diamond rows using med pink and following chart on page 7. Stitch two diamond Row A and two diamond Row B.

Work the end motif, Rows 1—27 as charted. Turn cloth top to bottom. Stitch the remaining half of the center motif, the same number of diamond rows, and the end motif.

If necessary, trim ends of cloth so the same number of rows border the end motifs at the top and bottom. Finish edges as desired; several methods are described on page 8.

Row	Length	Color	Row	Length	Color	Row	Length	Color
Center Motif			*End Motif*			14	2½W	lt pink
1	2¼W	dk pink	1	4W	dk pink	15	2½W	lt pink
2	2¼W	med pink	2	3W	med pink	16	2½W	med pink
3	2¼W	lt pink	3	2¼W	lt pink	17	2¾W	dk pink
4	3W	med pink	4	2½W	med pink	18	3W	dk pink
5	4W	dk pink	5	3W	dk pink	19	2½W	med pink
			6	2¾W	dk pink	20	2¼W	lt pink
Diamond Section (see page 7)			7	2½W	med pink	21	3W	med pink
A	3W	med pink	8	2½W	lt pink	22	4W	dk pink
B	3W	med pink	9	2½W	lt pink	23	1½W	dk pink
			10	2½W	med pink	24	2¾W	med pink
			11	2W	dk pink	25	2¾W	med pink
			12	2W	dk pink	26	3¾W	dk pink
			13	2½W	med pink	27	1½W	dk pink

Color Key
✖	center knot
——	lt pink
▬	med pink
▬▬	dk pink

Center Motif (one half)

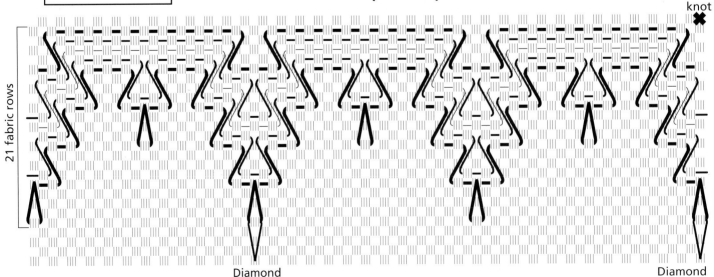

center knot

21 fabric rows

Diamond
Row A

Diamond
Row A

End Motif

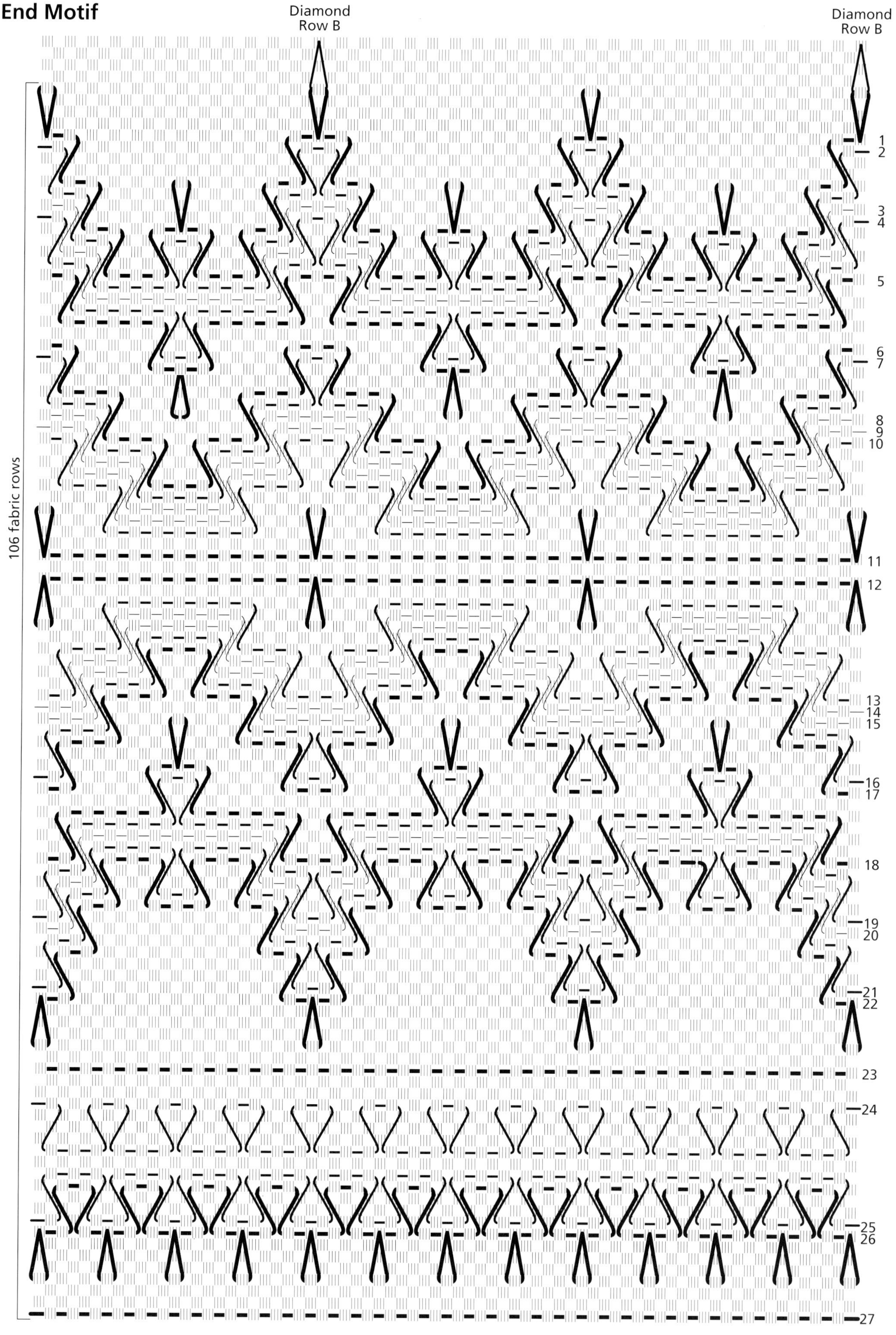

Diamond Row B
Diamond Row B
106 fabric rows
1
2
3
4
5
6
7
8
9
10
11
12
13
14
15
16
17
18
19
20
21
22
23
24
25
26
27

Crystalline

MATERIALS FOR A LARGE AFGHAN
two yards monk's cloth
lavender, med blue, and dk blue worsted weight
yarn (one 3 ounce skein of each color)
#13 metal yarn needle
measuring tape
safety pin
scissors

INSTRUCTIONS
Prepare monk's cloth as described on page 3. For a smaller afghan, refer to page 6 to plan the number of diamond rows needed. From the center knot, half of the center motif uses 17 fabric rows and the end motifs each use 105 fabric rows.

Place center knot over a block of horizontal threads; see page 4. Start with lavender yarn and stitch Row 1 of center motif. Stop stitching at the side a few rows from the hem and hide yarn end as described on page 4 (see Photo C). Stop in same place in the pattern on the opposite side.

After stitching Rows 1—5 of the center motif, stitch the diamond rows using lt blue and following chart on page 7. Stitch two diamond Row A and two diamond Row B.

Work the end motif, Rows 1—34 as charted. Turn cloth top to bottom. Stitch the remaining half of the center motif, the same number of diamond rows, and the end motif.

If necessary, trim ends of cloth so the same number of rows border the end motifs at the top and bottom. Finish edges as desired; several methods are described on page 8.

Row	Length	Color	Row	Length	Color	Row	Length	Color
Center Motif			*End Motif*			17	1³/₄W	lavender
1	2W	lavender	1	3¹/₂W	dk blue	18	1³/₄W	lavender
2	2¹/₂W	lavender	2	3¹/₄W	med blue	19	2W	dk blue
3	2¹/₂W	med blue	3	2¹/₂W	med blue	20	2W	med blue
4	3¹/₄W	med blue	4	2¹/₂W	lavender	21	2W	med blue
5	3¹/₂W	dk blue	5	2¹/₂W	lavender	22	2W	lavender
			6	2¹/₂W	med blue	23	2¹/₄W	lavender
Diamond Section (see page 7)			7	2¹/₂W	med blue	24	2¹/₄W	med blue
A	3W	med blue	8	2¹/₂W	dk blue	25	2¹/₄W	med blue
B	3W	med blue	9	2¹/₄W	dk blue	26	2¹/₄W	dk blue
			10	2¹/₄W	med blue	27	2¹/₂W	dk blue
			11	2¹/₄W	med blue	28	2¹/₂W	med blue
			12	2¹/₄W	lavender	29	2¹/₂W	med blue
			13	2W	lavender	30	2¹/₂W	lavender
			14	2W	med blue	31	2¹/₂W	lavender
			15	2W	med blue	32	2¹/₂W	med blue
			16	2W	dk blue	33	3¹/₄W	med blue
						34	3¹/₂W	dk blue

Color Key
✖ center knot
—— lavender
—— med blue
—— dk blue

Center Motif (one half)

center knot

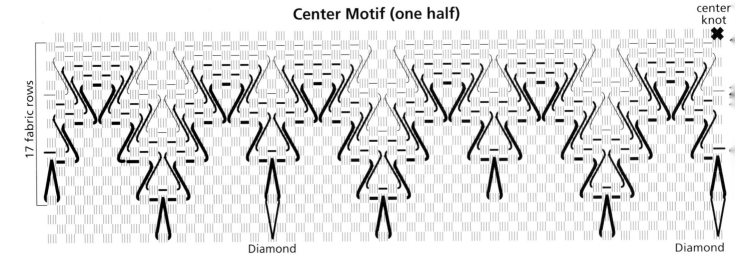

17 fabric rows

Diamond Row A

Diamond Row A

End Motif

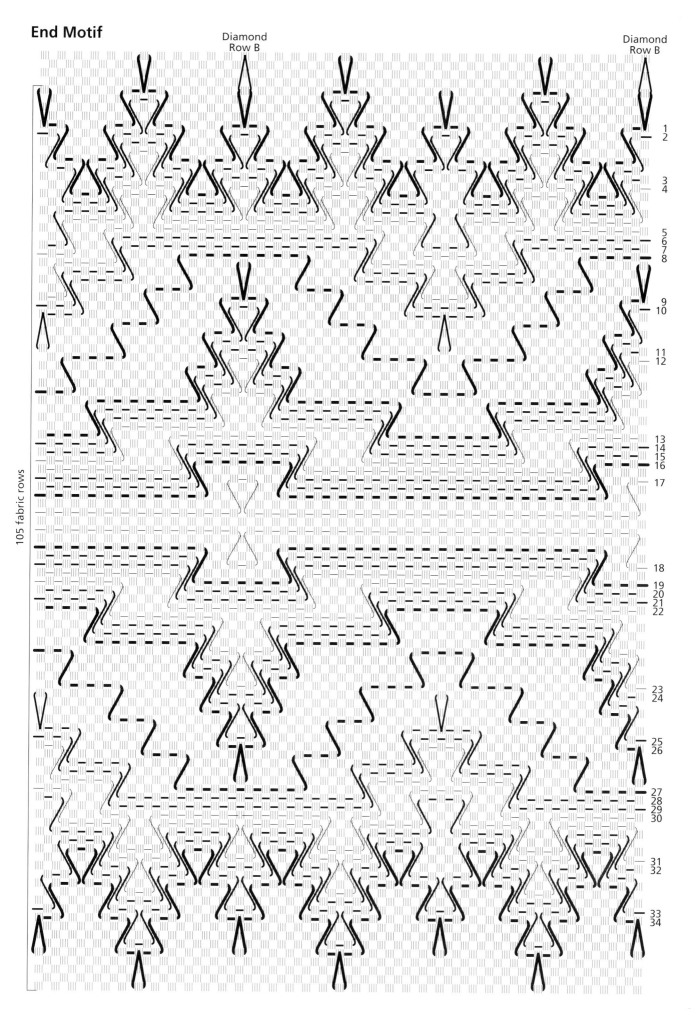

105 fabric rows

1
2
3
4
5
6
7
8
9
10
11
12
13
14
15
16
17
18
19
20
21
22
23
24
25
26
27
28
29
30
31
32
33
34

Pavé

MATERIALS FOR A SMALL THROW

one yard monk's cloth
lt blue, green, purple, and dk blue worsted weight
    yarn (one 3 ounce skein of each color)
#13 metal yarn needle
measuring tape
safety pin
scissors

INSTRUCTIONS

Prepare monk's cloth as described on page 3. For a larger afghan, refer to page 6 to plan the number of diamond rows needed. From the center knot, half of the center motif uses 16 fabric rows and the end motifs each use 81 fabric rows.

Place center knot over a block of vertical threads; see page 4. Start with lt blue yarn and stitch Row 1 of center motif. Stop stitching at the side a few rows from the hem and hide yarn end as described on page 4 (see Photo C). Stop in same place in the pattern on the opposite side.

After stitching Rows 1—4 of the center motif, stitch the diamond rows using lt blue and following chart on page 7. Stitch one diamond Row A and one diamond Row B.

Work the end motif, Rows 1—24 as charted. Turn cloth top to bottom. Stitch the remaining half of the center motif, the same number of diamond rows, and the end motif.

If necessary, trim ends of cloth so the same number of rows border the end motifs at the top and bottom. Finish edges as desired; several methods are described on page 8.

Row	Length	Color	Row	Length	Color	Row	Length	Color
Center Motif			*End Motif*			12	2W	dk blue
1	2W	lt blue	1	3¼W	dk blue	13	2W	dk blue
2	2W	green	2	3W	purple	14	2W	purple
3	3W	purple	3	2W	green	15	3W	green
4	3¼W	dk blue	4	2W	lt blue	16	3¼W	lt blue
			5	2W	lt blue	17	3¼W	dk blue
Diamond Section (see page 7)			6	2W	green	18	3W	purple
A	3W	lt blue	7	3W	purple	19	2W	green
B	3W	lt blue	8	3¼W	dk blue	20	2W	lt blue
			9	3¼W	lt blue	21	2W	lt blue
			10	3W	green	22	2W	green
			11	2W	purple	23	3W	purple
						24	3¼W	dk blue

Color Key
✖ center knot
——— lt blue
▬▬ green
▬▬ purple
▬▬ dk blue

Center Motif (one half)

center knot

16 fabric rows

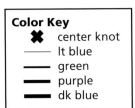

Diamond
Row A

Diamond
Row A

End Motif

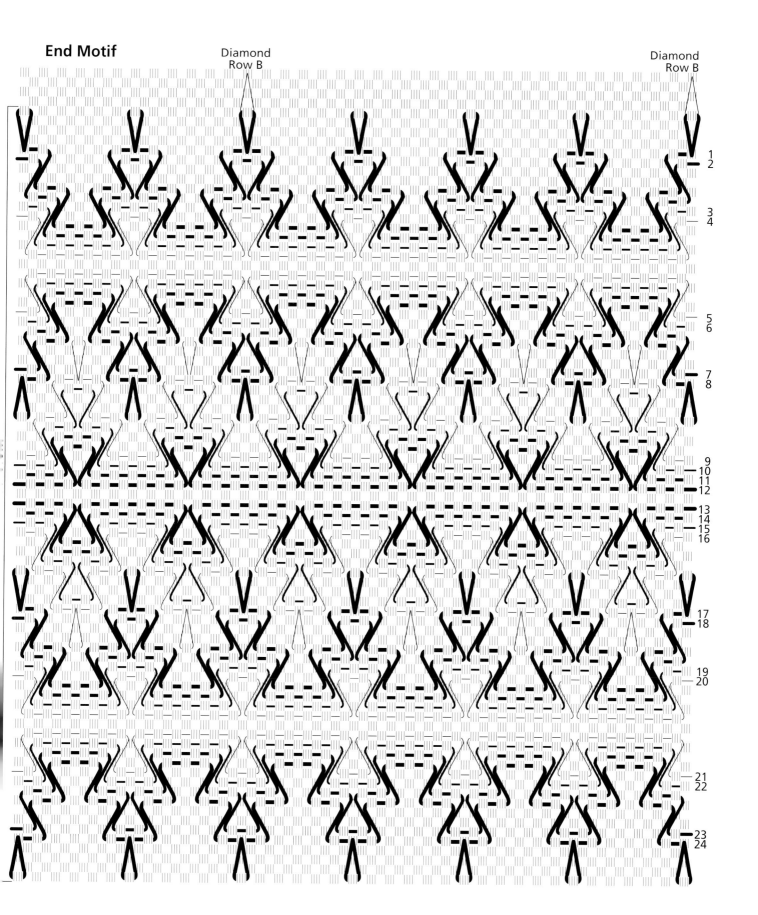

1
2

3
4

5
6

7
8

9
10
11
12

13
14
15
16

17
18

19
20

21
22

23
24

Solitaire — *2nd Did - 2013*

MATERIALS FOR A LARGE AFGHAN

two yards monk's cloth

lt green, med green, and dk green worsted weight
     yarn (one 3 ounce skein of each color)

#13 metal yarn needle

measuring tape

safety pin

scissors

INSTRUCTIONS

Prepare monk's cloth as described on page 3. For a smaller afghan, refer to page 6 to plan the number of diamond rows needed. From the center knot, half of the center motif uses 17 fabric rows and the end motifs each use 103 fabric rows.

Important: For this pattern, the diamond rows are shifted off center with relation to the center knot. The charts for the center and end motifs depict the V stitches for the diamond rows as a guide to placement.

Place center knot over a block of horizontal threads;

see page 4. Start with dk green yarn and stitch Row 1 of center motif. Stop stitching at the side a few rows from the hem and hide yarn end as described on page 4 (see Photo C). Stop in same place in the pattern on the opposite side.

After stitching Rows 1—4 of the center motif, stitch the diamond rows using lt green and following chart on page 7. Be sure the rows are positioned correctly. Stitch two diamond Row A and two diamond Row B.

Work the end motif, Rows 1—26 as charted. Turn cloth top to bottom. Stitch the remaining half of the center motif, the same number of diamond rows, and the end motif.

If necessary, trim ends of cloth so the same number of rows border the end motifs at the top and bottom. Finish edges as desired; several methods are described on page 8.

Row	Length	Color
Center Motif		
1	$1^3/4$W	dk green
2	$2^1/2$W	lt green
3	3W	med green
4	$3^1/4$W	dk green
Diamond Section (see page 7)		
A	3W	lt green
B	3W	lt green

Color Key

✖	center knot
——	lt green
——	med green
——	dk green

Row	Length	Color
End Motif		
1	$3^1/2$W	dk green
2	$3^1/4$W	med green
3	$2^3/4$W	lt green
4	$1^1/2$W	dk green
5	$2^1/4$W	lt green
6	$2^1/2$W	med green
7	$2^3/4$W	dk green
8	$3^1/4$W	dk green
9	$3^1/4$W	med green
10	$3^1/4$W	med green
11	$3^1/4$W	lt green
12	$3^1/2$W	lt green

Row	Length	Color
13	$3^1/2$W	med green
14	$3^1/2$W	med green
15	$3^3/4$W	dk green
16	$3^3/4$W	med green
17	$3^3/4$W	lt green
18	$3^1/4$W	dk green
19	3W	med green
20	$2^1/2$W	lt green
21	$1^1/2$W	dk green
22	$3^3/4$W	dk green
23	$3^1/4$W	med green
24	$3^1/4$W	med green
25	$3^3/4$W	dk green
26	$1^1/2$W	dk green

Center Motif (one half)

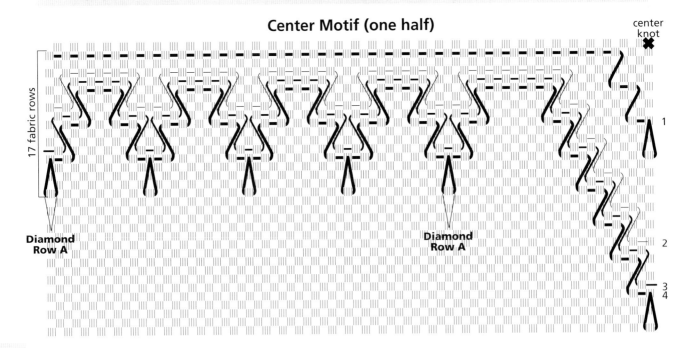

center knot

17 fabric rows

Diamond Row A

Diamond Row A

1

2

3
4

End Motif

103 fabric rows

1
2
3
4
5
6
7
8
9
10
11
12
13
14
15
16
17
18
19
20
21
22
23
24
25
26

Precious Gem

MATERIALS FOR A LARGE AFGHAN

two yards monk's cloth
white, lt blue, med blue, and dk blue worsted
      weight yarn (one 3 ounce skein of each color)
#13 metal yarn needle
measuring tape
safety pin
scissors

INSTRUCTIONS

Prepare monk's cloth as described on page 3. For a smaller afghan, refer to page 6 to plan the number of diamond rows needed. From the center knot, half of the center motif uses 21 fabric rows and the end motifs each use 103 fabric rows.

Place center knot over a block of horizontal threads; see page 4. Start with lt blue yarn and stitch Row 1

of center motif. Stop stitching at the side a few rows from the hem and hide yarn end as described on page 4 (see Photo C). Stop in same place in the pattern on the opposite side.

After stitching Rows 1—4 of the center motif, stitch the diamond rows using med blue and following chart on page 7. Stitch two diamond Row A and two diamond Row B.

Work the end motif, Rows 1—36 as charted. Turn cloth top to bottom. Stitch the remaining half of the center motif, the same number of diamond rows, and the end motif.

If necessary, trim ends of cloth so the same number of rows border the end motifs at the top and bottom. Finish edges as desired; several methods are described on page 8.

Row	Length	Color	Row	Length	Color			
Center Motif			*End Motif*			18	2W	lt blue
1	2W	lt blue	1	3¼W	white	19	2W	white
2	3W	med blue	2	3¼W	dk blue	20	2W	lt blue
3	3¼W	dk blue	3	3W	med blue	21	2W	med blue
4	3¼W	white	4	2W	lt blue	22	2W	dk blue
			5	1½W	white	23	2W	white
Diamond Section (see page 7)			6	1½W	dk blue	24	2¼W	dk blue
A	3W	med blue	7	2W	med blue	25	2¼W	med blue
B	3W	med blue	8	2¼W	white	26	2¼W	lt blue
			9	2¼W	dk blue	27	2¼W	lt blue
			10	2¼W	med blue	28	2¼W	med blue
			11	2¼W	lt blue	29	2¼W	dk blue
			12	2¼W	lt blue	30	2¼W	white
			13	2¼W	med blue	31	2W	med blue
			14	2¼W	dk blue	32	2W	dk blue
			15	2W	white	33	1½W	white
			16	2W	dk blue	34	1½W	lt blue
			17	2W	med blue	35	2¼W	med blue
						36	3¼W	white
			Row	**Length**	**Color**			

Color Key

✖ center knot
— white
— lt blue
— med blue
— dk blue

Center Motif (one half)

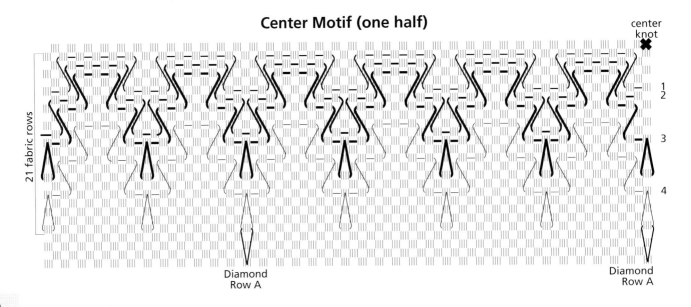

center knot

21 fabric rows

1
2
3
4

Diamond Row A

Diamond Row A

End Motif

103 fabric rows

1
2
3
4
5
6
7
8
9
10
11
12
13
14
15
16
17
18
19
20
21
22
23
24
25
26
27
28
29
30
31
32
33
34
35
36

21

Brilliance

MATERIALS FOR A LARGE AFGHAN
two yards monk's cloth
med teal, dk teal, and dk blue worsted weight yarn
(one 3 ounce skein of each color)
#13 metal yarn needle
measuring tape
safety pin
scissors

INSTRUCTIONS
Prepare monk's cloth as described on page 3. For a smaller afghan, refer to page 6 to plan the number of diamond rows needed. From the center knot, half of the center motif uses 30 fabric rows and the end motifs each use 97 fabric rows.

Place center knot over a block of vertical threads; see page 4. Start with med teal yarn and stitch Row 1 of center motif. Stop stitching at the side a few rows from the hem and hide yarn end as described on page 4 (see Photo C). Stop in same place in the pattern on the opposite side.

After stitching Rows 1—6 of the center motif, stitch the diamond rows using med teal and following chart on page 7. Stitch two diamond Row A and two diamond Row B.

Work the end motif, Rows 1—16 as charted. Turn cloth top to bottom. Stitch the remaining half of the center motif, the same number of diamond rows, and the end motif.

If necessary, trim ends of cloth so the same number of rows border the end motifs at the top and bottom. Finish edges as desired; several methods are described on page 8.

Row	Length	Color	Row	Length	Color	Row	Length	Color
Center Motif			*End Motif*			10	2¼W	med teal
1	2¼W	med teal	1	4W	dk blue	11	2½W	dk teal
2	2½W	dk teal	2	3¾W	dk teal	12	3¼W	dk blue
3	3¼W	dk blue	3	3½W	med teal	13	3¼W	med teal
4	3¼W	med teal	4	3½W	dk blue	14	3¼W	dk teal
5	3¼W	dk teal	5	3¼W	dk teal	15	3½W	dk blue
6	3½W	dk blue	6	3¼W	med teal	16	4W	dk blue
			7	3¼W	dk blue			
Diamond Section (see page 7)			8	2½W	dk teal			
A	3W	med teal	9	2¼W	med teal			
B	3W	med teal						

Color Key
✖ center knot
— med teal
— dk teal
— dk blue

Center Motif (one half)

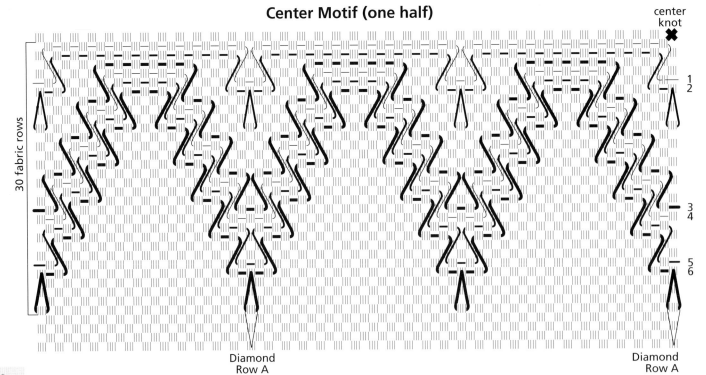

center knot

30 fabric rows

1
2

3
4

5
6

Diamond Row A

Diamond Row A

End Motif

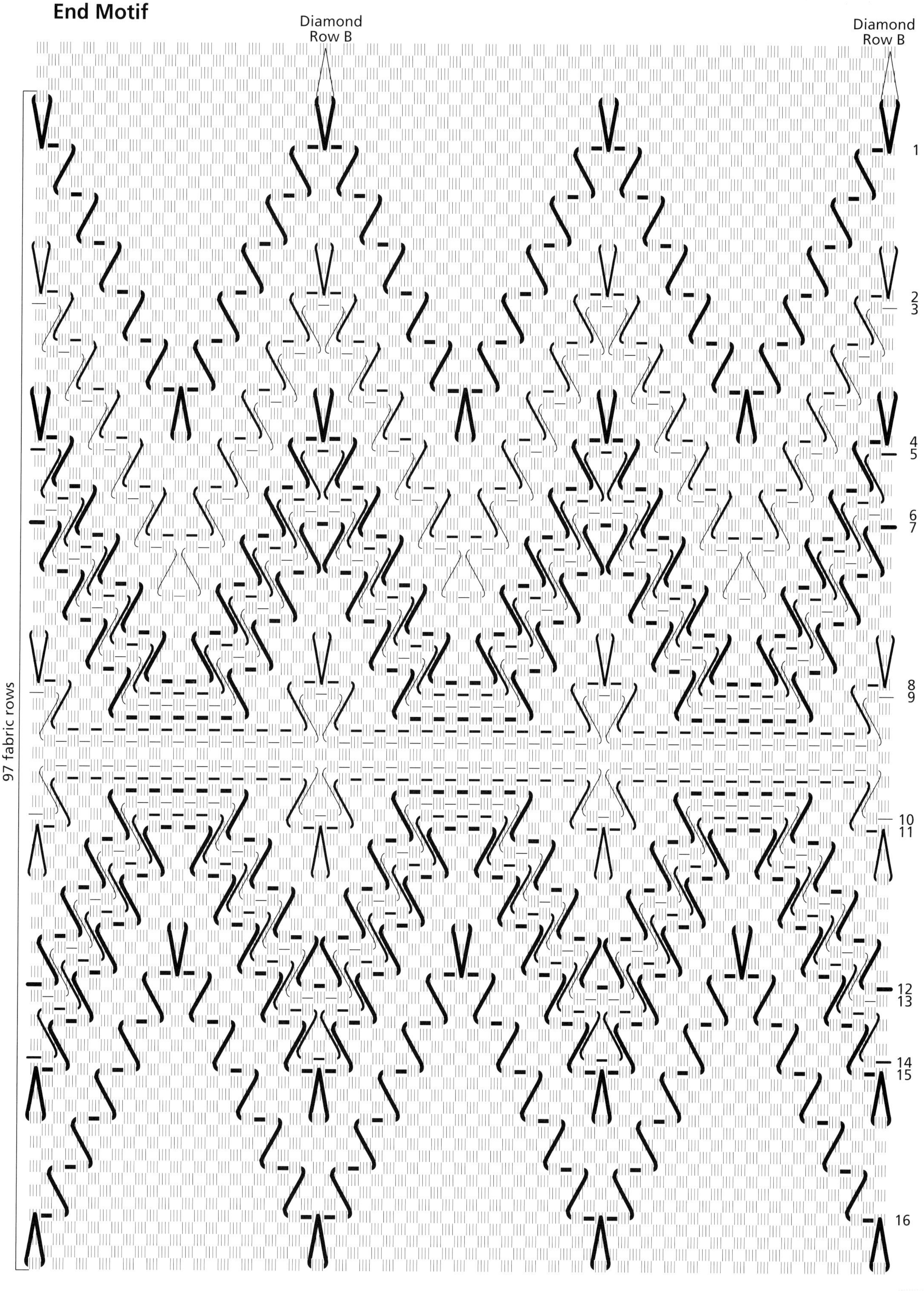
Diamond
Row B
Diamond
Row B
97 fabric rows
1
2
3
4
5
6
7
8
9
10
11
12
13
14
15
16

Dazzling

MATERIALS FOR A LARGE AFGHAN
two yards monk's cloth
peach, rust, med red, and dk red worsted weight
     yarn (one 3 ounce skein of each color)
#13 metal yarn needle
measuring tape
safety pin
scissors

INSTRUCTIONS
Prepare monk's cloth as described on page 3. For a smaller afghan, refer to page 6 to plan the number of diamond rows needed. From the center knot, half of the center motif uses 25 fabric rows and the end motifs each use 99 fabric rows.

Place center knot over a block of horizontal threads; see page 4. Start with dk red yarn and stitch Row 1 of center motif. Stop stitching at the side a few rows from the hem and hide yarn end as described on page 4 (see Photo C). Stop in same place in the pattern on the opposite side.

After stitching Rows 1—5 of the center motif, stitch the diamond rows using med red and following chart on page 7. Stitch two diamond Row A and two diamond Row B.

Work the end motif, Rows 1—26 as charted. Turn cloth top to bottom. Stitch the remaining half of the center motif, the same number of diamond rows, and the end motif.

If necessary, trim ends of cloth so the same number of rows border the end motifs at the top and bottom. Finish edges as desired; several methods are described on page 8.

Row	Length	Color	Row	Length	Color	Row	Length	Color
Center Motif			*End Motif*			13	2¼W	peach
1	2W	dk red	1	3¼W	dk red	14	2¼W	peach
2	2½W	peach	2	3¼W	med red	15	2¼W	peach
3	2½W	rust	3	3W	rust	16	2½W	rust
4	3W	med red	4	3¼W	peach	17	2½W	rust
5	3½W	dk red	5	3¼W	dk red	18	2¾W	med red
			6	3¼W	dk red	19	2¾W	med red
Diamond Section (see page 7)			7	3¼W	dk red	20	3¼W	dk red
A	3W	med red	8	2¾W	med red	21	3¼W	dk red
B	3W	dk red	9	2¾W	med red	22	3½W	dk red
			10	2½W	rust	23	3W	med red
			11	2½W	rust	24	2½W	rust
			12	2¼W	peach	25	2½W	peach
						26	2W	dk red

Color Key
✖ center knot
— peach
— rust
— med red
— dk red

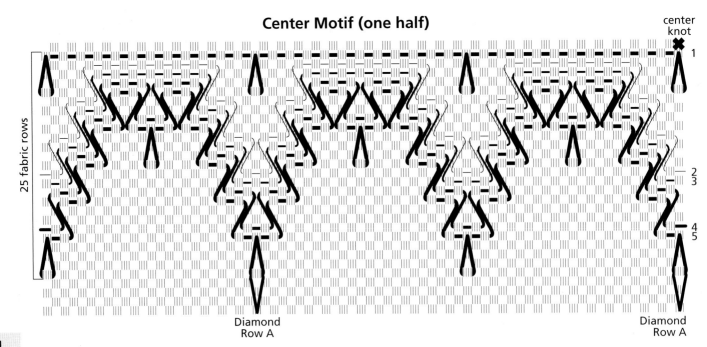

Center Motif (one half)

center knot

25 fabric rows

Diamond Row A

Diamond Row A